ISBN 978-1-907094-66-8

BR BRUSH CLASS 47

48 YEARS OF DIFFERENT LIVERIES

Back in the latter 1950's when the BR Board took the decision to replace the steam locomotives with diesels, some hasty decisions were taken, resulting in orders being placed for untested designs, which in many cases developed into financial as well as technical disasters. Many of these were in the Class 1 & 2 category, whereas the type 4's (Class 40 & 44's), especially the Class 40's proved to be too heavy at around 133 tons relative to their power capabilities at 2000hp. Both designs also suffering from the 1-Co-Co-1 wheel arrangement, which tended to cause problems on poorly maintained track in marshalling yards.

A requirement for a Co-Co design, weighing around 115 tons and with an output of 2750hp was considered to be the correct combination for a design capable of being able to travel over most of the network, and which would be able to haul express passenger, heavy freight and local services.

Brush won the order against the competition, initially for 20 locomotives, with the first example (No D1500) appearing from the Brush Works at Loughborough in an attractive dual green livery in the summer of 1962. Initially No. D1500 crew training was carried out between Kings Cross-Cambridge and Hull, followed by dynamometer car tests from London Kings Cross to Doncaster. No D1501 was loaned to the Western Region for tests and soon returned to Finsbury Park depot, where the locomotives were based, with crew training then taking place at Leeds Neville Hill, Sheffield Darnell, Edinburgh Haymarket, so by the summer of 1963 they were available for freight work on the ECML plus some of the main passenger duties ousting the Class 40's from such workings with the help of the Deltics and Class 46's. Production at Crewe resulted in the first example No. D1550 appearing in January 1964, by May 1968 there were 512 built, although there were never 512 in service at the same time as Nos D1734 and D1671 were written off due to accident damage before No. D1961 was completed.

They have often been described as the Standard Type 4's, but this is far from the case, there being over the years sub-classes from 47/0's to 47/9's, with variations within the sub-classes. The Class 47/3's had no heating capabilities and so were mainly freight locomotives, but were frequently seen on passenger work in the summer months.

The Class didn't achieve the availability figures that had been hoped for, and suffered problems, some which were quite expensive to rectify during their early years, resulting in them being derated from 2750hp to 2580hp. In 1976 a 5 year refurbishment program was started, which resulted in better performance figures.

5 members of the Class Nos D1702-D1706 had the Sulzer Vee-type 12 cylinder 12LVA24 engine fitted rated at 2650hp. They were known as the Class 48, and initially allocated to Shirebrook for freight work. In due course they moved to the Great Eastern line before returning to Tinsley in 1970. Being non standard they were eventually returned to Class 47/0's.

This album has been completed to show the majority of the main liveries carried over the years, some sources say there have been 300 variations others just over 200, but whatever the figure there are far too many to illustrate individually, but it is quite a thought that at one time the Class was all in the BR blue with or without the large logo, since those days most of the variations have occurred.

If you require technical details about the Class, then I would strongly recommend Sulzer Diesel Locomotives of British Rail by Brian Webb published in 1977 by David & Charles or for up to date information Colin Marsden's Locomotives Illustrated parts 180 & 181.

As the Class approaches 50 years since its introduction, there are still around 60 examples in existence, most of which are in operation either on preserved lines or on the network where they can still be seen working freight as well as passenger services.

When there were over 500 Class 47's in service, they tended to be taken for granted by enthusiasts especially when they were virtually all in the BR blue livery, but they have outlived many classes eg. 56, 50, 58 which were introduced after them, and in 2011 they are still to be seen almost every day of the year at work somewhere on the network.

I hope the album will provide a pleasant reminder of some of the liveries the class has carried, from the more sombre examples to the most eye catching, but no doubt in the next few years there will probably be more variations.

Gavin Morrison, January 2011

Front Cover Picture: Date 8th September 2004. Class 47/8 No. 47810 Porterbrook heads the morning Euston-Holyhead express along the North Wales Coast approaching Peamaenmaur.
Gavin Morrison

Back Cover Picture: Date 21st April 2010. As a result of the disastrous floods caused by the River Derwent that hit Workington and the surrounding areas on 19th November 2009 when the Calva main road bridge across the river collapsed, DRS and Northern Rail combined with the DFT to run a shuttle service of 12 round trips per day (7.20am to 19.15pm) free of charge between Workington and Maryport, and network rail constructed a temporary station, known as Workington north at Siddick just across the river, with unheard of speed. The whole operation was a huge success and much credit must be given to all concerned. DRS provided a variety of Motive Power, which included 37's, 57's, 47's and even a Class 20. One the date I visited 2 immaculate 47's, Nos 47501 'Craftsman' and 47832 'Galloway Princess' were working the service, which is shown approaching Workington Derwent Junction surrounded by very colourful gorse bushes. Details of 47501 and 47832 have been given on pages 66 and 54.

First published in the United Kingdom by Book Law Publications 2011, 382 Carlton Hill, Nottingham, NG4 1JA
Printed and bound by The Amadeus Press, Cleckheaton, West Yorkshire

Date: 26.9.1964
The reason for me being at Grayrigg station (closed on 1st February 1954) was nothing to do with the passage of new Class 47 No. D1624, built at Crewe, but not in BR service until the following month, but to see the last train on BR hauled by the last Princes Coronation No. 46256 'Sir William Stanier FRS'. Crewe Works used to send the new locomotives out on test runs over Shap, usually still only painted in undercoat. It was allocated to the Midland, Western, Eastern and North Eastern Regions, being renumbered 47043 in February 1974, followed by 47566 in May 1980. It suffered accident damage in May 1981 which was repaired at Stratford, where it also received the silver roof treatment from the depot. It was withdrawn in October 1994 in Inter-city (not swallow) livery and scrapped at Booth-Roe Metals at Rotherham in March 2006. *Gavin Morrison*

Date 2nd July 1966
No. D1999 had only been released by Crewe Works the previous month, before the picture was taken of it leaving Bradford Exchange with a train for Kings Cross. The locomotive stands out well against the soot encrusted wall. Bradford Exchange was replaced by a new station in January 1973, 200 yards to the south, which became Bradford Interchange in May 1983.

No. D1999 started it's career allocated to York and was re-numbered to No. 47297 in February 1974 which it retained to the end of it's career which came in February 1999. It carried the name 'Cobra Railfreight' between May 1995 and March 1999. It became part of the Railfreight Distribution fleet in it's latter years, and was not scrapped until April 2002, this was done by a private company, and was not deleted from the records until July 2002, but was never officially recorded as withdrawn. *Gavin Morrison*

Date 29th April 1967

No. D1103 was part of the last batch of 47's to be built at Crewe, and did not enter service until October 1966, when it was sent to York Depot. In its steam heat fitted days it is approaching Wortley Junction South at Leeds with the up 'Yorkshire Pullman' comprising of 7 Metro-Cammell Pullman cars with a Mark 1 BG in blue and grey in the middle. The background above the train was once the site of the former steam engine shed of Copley Hill. No. D1103 spent virtually it's entire career on the Eastern and North Eastern regions working East Coast Main line expresses. It changed identities in March 1974 becoming a Class 47/4 and numbered 47520 after the fitting of ETH (electric train heating). It ended it's days in Inter City Main line livery with the very small numbers and was withdrawn in August 1998. It carried the name 'Thunderbird' between November 1993 and July 1994, and was very often to be seen at King's Cross on these duties.

Gavin Morrison

Date 29th May 1972
A busy scene in Edinburgh Princes Street Gardens as No. 1575 in the blue livery but with the arrow emblems behind the cab doors. It is heading the down 1551 which was the 7.20 from York to Aberdeen. On the right of the picture is Haymarkets Class 40 No. D265.

No. 1575 became No. 47455 in February 1974, and spent most of its career allocated to Eastern and LM Region. A spell at Stratford shed in 1988 saw it receive the silver roof treatment, but it's career came to a premature end in November 1989 when it was involved in an accident at Headcorn near Ashford which resulted in withdrawal in March 1990, although it was not scrapped until June 1995.

Gavin Morrison

Date 3rd September 1977

The south end of Aberdeen station used to have some impressive signal gantries, sadly they have long sincegone. Here Class 47/4 No. 47418 powers out of the Granite City heading the 8.45am to Glasgow Queen Street. It was one of the first batch of Class 47's to be built by Brush and entered service in March 1963, this batch of 21 Class 47's (Nos D1500 to D1520) were known as the 'Generators', the auxillary generator was for Electric Train heating, this was only fitted to this batch. No. 47418 was allocated to the Eastern and North Eastern Regions and received a general overhaul in March 1985 and it continued in service until February 1991 and scrapped in December 1995. It was one of the relatively few members of the class 47/4 to retain the blue livery until withdrawal. It's original number was D1517. *Gavin Morrison*

(Top Left)

Date 19 February 1978

No. 47163 is seen at Crewe Works, complete with the Union Jack it received by Stratford depot to commemorate the Queen's Silver Jubilee in 1977. No. 47164 received similar treatment. The loco carried many different numbers, starting with D1757 when new in September 1964. No. 47163 was allocated in February 1974, then 47610 in April 1984, followed by 47823 in April 1989, and finally 47787 when it became part of the Rail Express Systems fleet (RES) in November 1994. It was involved in a serious accident at Kensal Green in December 1977 and was badly burnt as can be seen in the picture. It was out of service until July 1979. It was named 'SS Great Britain' in October 1992 then 'Victim Support' in December 1994 and finally Windsor Castle in April 2002 for 2 years when it was frequently used on Royal Train duties by EWS. Its interesting career still continues as part of the West Coast Fleet. *Gavin Morrison*

(Bottom)

Date 25th July 1981

Nos. 47711 and 47712 were the first of the class to receive the large arrow livery, which transformed their appearance from the previously drab BR blue with small arrow. Both are seen on Haymarket depot at Edinburgh where they were members of the class 47/7 fleet, fitted with push and pull for working the shuttle services to Glasgow Queen Street from Edinburgh Waverley and later to Aberdeen. No. 47711 entered service from Brush Works as No. D1941 in June 1966, becoming No. 47498 in February 1974, and 47711 in September 1979. It carried the name 'Greyfriars Bobby' from April 1981 to December 1990, and then 'County of Hertfordshire' between July 1993 and 2000 when it became part of the Network South East fleet. It was withdrawn June 2000 by EWS. *Gavin Morrison*

Date 5 September 1980

Apart from Nos. 47711 and 47712, the Class 47/7's remained in the standard BR blue livery, but in some cases with a white roof. Here No. 47709, named 'The Lord Provost' in September 1979 heads a diverted 11.30 Glasgow Queen Street – Edinburgh Waverley past Greenhill Junction at Bonneybridge. The locomotive was new from Brush as D1942 in June 1966, and was a London Midland locomotive until May 1973 when it moved to the Western Region. It arrived at the Scottish Region for push-pull duties in May 1978, but moved to Network South East in October 1990. It was bought by Pete Waterman in May 1994, then sold to Fragonset in January 1997. It worked for the Blue Pullman Co. during the companies short existence and was named 'Dionysis' between August 2001 and February 2007. Happily after it's unstable existence in private ownership, it's now part of the Direct Rail Services (DRS) fleet.

Gavin Morrison

Date 8th May 1982
During the 1970's and 1980's Stratford Depot had a reputation for the smartest Class 47's on the BR network most of which received the silver roofs. No. 47583 seems to have been a depot favourite as it received a special one off large logo blue livery in 1981 to mark the wedding of HRH the 'Prince of Wales' to Lady Diana Spencer, after which it got the standard large logo blue, which is shown in this picture of it leaving Chesterfield at the head of the Manchester Piccadilly-Harwich boat train. It started as No. D1767 in October 1964, then 47172 in March 1974, followed by 47583 in November 1980 and finally 47734 when it became part of the Rail Express Systems Fleet. It was named 'County of Hertfordshire' in July 1979 and then 'Crewe Diesel Depot' Quality Approved in March 1996. It carried the Network South East livery as well as the RES. It was withdrawn in February 2004, but not scrapped until May 2008 by European Metal Reprocessing at Kingsbury.
Gavin Morrison

21st May 1987
The Scottish Class 47/7's started to receive the Inter-City livery in mid 1985, but the red stripe along the bodyside was replaced by blue one, and Scot Rail replaced Inter-City. All except No. 47716 received appropriate Scottish names. Nos. 47702 'Saint Cuthbert' and 47708 'Waverley' are both ready to leave Glasgow Queen Street, 47702 on the 17.25 to Dyce, and 47708 on the 1600 to Waverley. No. 47702 nearest the camera entered service as No. D1947 from Brush in July 1966 and went to the LM Region until December 1972, when it was operated by the Western Region until arriving in Scotland in December 1978. It became No. 47504 in March 1974 until receiving 47702 in March 1979. After it's use on the push pull services ended it moved to Network South East in May 1990 and was named 'County of Suffolk' between February 1994 and October 1998. Its career ended in April 2000, and it was scrapped at Toton in January 2005.
Gavin Morrison

Date 21st May 1987
To mark the 150th Anniversary of the Great Western Railway in 1985, the Western Region repainted 4 Class 47's Nos. 47079, 47484, 47500 and 47628 into Great Western Green livery complete with brass number and nameplates. No. 47500 'Great Western' received it's name in February 1979. Together with No. 47484 'Isambard Kingdom Brunel' they were both kept in immaculate condition by Old Oak Common depot during the celebrations and afterwards, when they were frequently rostered for VSOE and Royal Train duties. On a rather less glamourous duty, No. 47500 'Great Western' emerges from Hillfield Tunnel at Newport heading 1M84 Cardiff-Crewe passenger train. Even before the GW celebrations No. 47500 was always well cared for by Old Oak Common. It was new as D1943 in June 1966 and went to the LM Region until March 1973, and then to the Western Region. By 1991 it was at Immingham depot minus Brass number and nameplates, and presented a sorry sight in it's patched green livery, spending much of it's time at Leeds hauling Class 91's between Leeds and Bradford Forster Square on the King's Cross services. It eventually was purchased by West Coast Railways and after many years out of use has been reinstated in 2010, unfortunately not in the Great Western Livery.
Gavin Morrison

(*Top Left*)

Date 23.4.88

A Network South East Class 47/4 on the 12.37 Carlisle Leeds service was very unusual. No. 47583 County of Hertfordshire' must have been heading back to Old Oak Common. It is passing Wortley Junction on the north side of Leeds. It started life as D1767 in October 1964, became No. 47172 in February 1974 then 47583 in November 1980 and finally No. 47734 in March 1996 and named 'Quality Approved' in March 1996 when in the RES fleet and was withdrawn in February 2004. *Gavin Morrison*

(*Bottom*)

Date 15.4.88

Thornaby Depot in the North East was primarily for freight, and it had an allocation of the no-heat Class 47/3's, which it frequently modified the BR blue livery in the 1980's. No. 47361 is passing Burton Salmon with a tank train from Stanlow heading north. It has large numbers with a small logo, plus the depots Kingfisher badge, plus a yellow stripe along the base of the body. It entered traffic in February 1966 as No. D1880 and became 47361 in February 1974. It carried the name 'Wilton Endeavour' between July 1983 and October 1999, before it was withdrawn in May 2001. The lines to the left head for Pontefract and eventually Sheffield. *Gavin Morrison*

Date 6.5.1988
Class 47/4 No. 47522 was unique within the class as the only one to be painted in this attractive apple green livery. This was in connection with an open day at Doncaster Works on 3rd October 1987 when it was named 'Doncaster Enterprise'. It kept this livery for 3 years until it became part of the RES fleet. In May 1982 it was involved in a serious accident at 'Forteviot in Scotland, and was out of service until October 1983 after a rebuild. It was again involved in another accident in either December 1989 or January 1990 at Dover and repaired again It started as D1105 in November 1966, became No. 47522 in March 1974 eventually being officially withdrawn in RES livery in August 1998, although it is recorded as being scrapped in May 1998 in Rotherham. It is shown in this picture heading IM87, the 7.20 Harwich-Manchester Piccadilly boat train approaching Cowburn Tunel at the head of the Hope Valley in Derbyshire.

Gavin Morrison

Date 19th August 1989
Initially 6 Class 47/4's were painted in the Network South East colours for working the Great Eastern line services out of Liverpool Street. For the first 6 a light blue was used, but this was altered to a darker blue for the remainder of the 47's within the sector. Here No. 47596, named 'Aldeburgh Festival' in June 1984 heads the empty stock off the 9.00 ex Kings Lynn up Bethnal Green Bank out to the carriage sidings at Stratford. After the electrification of all the Great Eastern services the Class 47's were transferred to Old Oak Common for working the Newbury and Oxford trains and eventually replacing the Class 50's on the Waterloo-Exeter services. No. 47596 was new as No. D1933 in March 1966 and became 47255 in February 1974, and eventually No. 47596 in October 1983. It was allocated No. 47740 in the RES fleet but this never happened. Happily it was sold for preservation to the Stratford 47 group in January 2003 and can now be seen on the Mid Norfolk Railway. *Gavin Morrison*

Date 26 June 1989
To celebrate the 150th anniversary of the Midland Counties Railway in 1989, one of the BR Research Class 47's No. 97561 (formally 47561) was chosen to be repainted into this very attractive red livery and named Midland Counties 150 1839-1989. Unfortunately the names were removed in March 1990 and it was repainted into Inter-City livery in the summer. This picture of it was taken at Crewe depot. It was new as D1614 in August 1964, No. 47034 followed March 1974, 47561 in October 1980, 97561 in September 1988 and finally 47973 in July 1989. It carried a second name 'Derby Evening Telegraph' from September 1990 to September 1996, and was withdrawn in August 1996, and cut-up by February 1997.

B.G. Hughes

Date 31.8.1989
No. 47615 is shown at Holyhead ready to leave with 27 freightliner wagons for Basford Hall. This site is now a car park for the Irish Ferry traffic, although there has been talk recently of a possible re-opening. The locomotive carried no less than 4 different names starting (as seen here) with 'Caerphilly Castle' between April 1985 and August 1992 having been a Western Region locomotive until 1987. It was painted into the basic Railfreight grey livery but without any Freightliner decals. It passed into the RES fleet receiving the red livery and being numbered 47747 and named 'Res Publica' between June 1994 and June 2000. 'Graham Farish' name followed in August 2000 until September 2002 and finally 'Florence Nightingale' from October 2002 until May 2007. Its number history started with D1929 in February 1966, No. 47252 followed in March 1974, No. 47615 in June 1984 and finally 47747.

Date 31 August 1989
In the days of Container/Freightliner services out of Holyhead, Class 47/3 No. 47347 in Railfreight Distribution first livery approaches Rhyl with a service for Stratford in London. The locomotive entered service as No. D1828 in March 1965 and spent the first 10 years of it's career on mainly freight services on the London Midland Region. It became No. 47347 in April 1974 and continued in service until stored in December 1996. It was selected as being suitable for conversion to a Class 57/0 and emerged from Brush Works at Loughborough in October 1998 as No. 57004 in Freightliner green livery.

Gavin Morrison

Date 9th March 1990
One of the Class 47/3's to receive the Thornaby special painting treatment was No. 47363 which spent 6 years allocated to Thornaby between 1984 and 1990. Here it is seen with large white numbers and the distinctive 'Kingfisher' depot logo heading the 10.26 Weaste to Port Clarence through Horbury cutting, just to the east of Healey Mills yard. It was new in July 1965 as No. D1882, renumbered 47363 in February 1974, then 47385 in July 1999 and then back to 47363 in October 1995. It received the name 'Billingham Enterprise' at Darlington Station on 6 December 1985, which it carried until October 1991. It was stored February 1999, and eventually sold to Fragonset in September 2001 and is currently stored at West Coast Railways Carnforth.
Gavin Morrison

Date 23rd July 1990
No. 47575 was named 'City of Hereford' in June 1985. It was easily recognisable by having a yellow wrap round livery of the cabs and slightly larger numbers. Here it is working a van train past Monk Fryston heading for Bristol. It ended it's days in the parcels sector and was painted in the red livery. It was new as No. D1770 in October 1964, became No. 47175 in February 1974, and finally 47575 in March 1981. It was allocated No. 47730 in the RES fleet, but this did not happen. It was stored in February 2001 and was eventually used to provide spares for Riviera.
Gavin Morrison

Date 27th August 1990
After climbing the 3 miles of around 1m 40 from Aller Junction to Dainton summit, No. 47835 'Windsor Castle' in it's customary immaculate Inter-City livery bursts out of the tunnel at the summit, heading a Derby-Plymouth express. The locomotive spent almost 30 years allocated to the Western Region, starting as No. D1654 in January 1965, it changed to 47070 in February 1974 and then 47620 in September 1984. When converted to a class 47/8 it became No. 47835 receiving the name 'Windsor Castle' in July 1985, which it carried until May 1995, when with No. 47834 became the choice of locomotive for Royal Train Duties. The locomotives became part of the RES fleet, No. 47835 became 47799 in May 1995 and named 'Prince Henry' and painted in a claret livery with RES emblems. On the formation of EWS in 1996, the livery was altered in October 1997 with a thin yellow/red band across the middle of the body panels. Their royal train duties were taken over by Class 67's Nos. 67005 and 67006 in 2004. Both locomotives still exist, No. 47798 'Prince William' being in the National Collection.

Gavin Morrison

Date 27th August 1990
Carrying the Inter-City Swallow decal but no Inter-City branding No. 47826 arrives at Dainton Summit from Totnes at the head of the 10.00 Plymouth-Edinburgh. It started it's career in Scotland as No. D1976 in November 1965, changed to 47274 in September 1974 and became No. 47637 in January 1986 receiving the name 'Springburn' in June 1987 which it carried until November 1989, it also carried larger than normal white numbers on the cabside. When it became No. 47826 it lost it's name. The name was attached again in November 2001. Withdrawn in August 2002, when Virgin ceased to use 47's on their Cross Country trains, it passed to West Coast Railways where it is currently in use. *Gavin Morrison*

Date 15 September 1990
Devoid of all branding No. 47846 is shown leaving Teignmouth to run along the seafront at the head of the 8.45 Saturdays only Paignton-Liverpool. New to the Western Region in April 1965 as D1677 it changed to No. 47091 in March 1974. No. 47647 followed in April 1986 and finally 47846 in December 1989. It received the name 'Thor' off No. D1671, destroyed by an accident in 1966, and carried it from August 1966 until June 2002 having been withdrawn in May. It became part of the small Great Western fleet of 47/8's and painted in the dark green livery, and then the green 'First' livery when that company took over. In due course it was sent to Brush for rebuilding into a Virgin Class 57/3 as No. 57308 where it is currently still in use by Virgin for Thunderbird (rescue) duties.

Gavin Morrison

Date 13 October 1990
6 Class 47's were allocated to the BR Research department for test trains. When not employed on these duties they were available for other work. They were originally allocated numbers in the 97XXX series, but became 47971 to 47976 from July 1989. No. 47975 in the 'Dutch' departmental livery is working a railtour with No. 47549, along the docks branch at Hull. It had many identities starting as D1723 in March 1964, it was allocated No. 47132 but never carried it, became 47540 in October 1974, then 47975 in August 1990, returning to 47540 in December 1995. It carried the name 'The Institution of Civil Engineers' from September 1991 to June 1995. It was eventually purchased privately and stored just off the main A1 road near Thirsk, but became derelict. It was one of the few Class 47/4's to run in the Dutch livery.

Date 24th June 1991
No. 47286 recently repainted into the Railfreight Distribution first livery, is shown passing Eaglescliffe in the North East with an up freight. It entered service as No. D1988 in February 1966 and only had one number change to 47286 in February 1974. It was named 'Port of Liverpool' at Seaforth Dock in December 1993, continuing in service with RFD until stored in February 1999. It was scrapped in August 2000, but was never officially withdrawn.
Gavin Morrison

Date 15 August 1991
2 months before it received the name 'Resourceful' which it carried until January 2004, No. 47594 looks very smart in it's recently acquired RES livery, but before it became No. 47739 in July 1994. It is shown leaving Bradford Interchange with an evening van train. It was new in August 1964 as D1615, became No. 47035 in February 1974, then 47594 in September 1983 and finally 47739. It now carries the name 'Robin of Templecombe' which it received in September 2008, and is currently active in the Colas fleet. It was the first to receive the RES (Rail Express System Livery) and was painted at Swanwick.
Gavin Morrison

Date 11th July 1991
The pioneer Class 47 is shown in this picture, running in an imitation BR green livery, applied by Immingham depot, where for it's last few years it appears to have become the depot favourite and received special treatment, gaining the unofficial name 'Star of India' on 1st May 1991.

It first appeared from Brush Works at the beginning of September 1962 and went to Crewe Works for weighing returning to Brush. On 27th September 1962 it was taken into stock and on the following day work a Kings Cross-Hull train. Dynamometer Car trials followed. By October 1963 it was allocated to Tinsley, and the following year to Finsbury Park. It received the name 'North Eastern' in December 1981 which it carried until May 1988. It was sold to the '47401 Project' based at the Midland Railway Centre at Butterley where it arrived on 7th July 1993. It has been restored and can be frequently seen at work at this site.

Gavin Morrison

Date 11th July 1991
The Railfreight Petroleum sector had a fleet of 33 class 47's for working their heavy trains around the country. One of these was the Weaste to Port Clarence working which crossed the Pennines, and is shown here headed by No. 47119 in the cutting at Horbury just to the east of Healey Mills yard. The locomotive was originally No. D1708 when new in January 1964, becoming 47119 in May 1974. It was named 'Arcidae' in August 1988, but it came to a premature end after a collision with a road tanker at Billingham in May 1992, being withdrawn 1 week later. It was sold to Waterman Railways as a source of spares, eventually being scrapped in December 1995. *Gavin Morrison*

Date 7th March 1992

Well away for its usual Inter-City cross-country and other routes, No. 47811 in the Inter City Swallow livery passes Hall Royd Junction at Todmorden before tackling the climb to Copy Pit Summit. It is heading a North Eastern Locomotive Preservation Group Special (NELPG). The locomotive became part of the small fleet of 47/8's allocated to the Great Western Franchise from 1996, and then went to First Great Western when they took over 2 years later.

It was new as No. D1719 in February 1974, becoming No. 47239 in April 1974, then 47656 in September 1986 and 47811 in August 1989. It is currently part of the Freightliner fleet, but has not been in main line service for some time.

Gavin Morrison

Date 27th August 2001
When the First Group took over the Great Western Franchise in 1998, it altered the livery. The small number of Class 47/8's were changed to the green livery shown here on number 47832, which is seen passing Slough at the head of the 8.20 Penzance-Paddington.

No. 47832 was unusual in that it was only ever allocated to the Western Region in BR days, but since privatisation it has been owned by Great Western, First, Fragonset, and is current in use with Direct Rail Services. It was new in August 1964 and numbered D1610, then it became No. 47031 in April 1974, 47560 in July 1980 finally 47832 in June 1989. It was named 'Tamar' from April 1982 until May 2001 although the plates were removed for 1 month in 1994. 'Driver Tom Clark OBE' from September 2005 to June 2007, and is currently named 'Solway Princess'.

Gavin Morrison

Date 28th August 2002
As part of an anti-trespass campaign in March 2002, Virgin and the BT Police had No. 47829 painted in this smart livery. It operated Cross Country services so was seen over most of the network. Class 37 No. 37093 had similar treatment in 1985 and operated in the North East, whether or not it did any good has never really been established. It is shown inside Liverpool Lime Street having just arrived on the 6.40am from Poole. After being used by Freightliner, it was sold to Riviera Trains, then Harry Needle Railroad Co. and then DRS, after which Harry Needle bought it back. It is currently (Dec. 2010) at Long Marston stored. It started as No. D1964 when new in September 1965, then became No. 47264 in July 1874, followed by 47619 in August 1984 and finally 47829 in June 1989. It has never carried a name. *Gavin Morrison*

Date 15th July 2002
Only a few Class 47's received the Freightliner green livery. As well as hauling the liner trains they occasionally appeared on empty stock duties and general freight but appearances on passenger workings were rare. No. 47150 is shown in this picture heading north along the West Coast Main line at Kenton, on the 6M46 14.20 Tilbury to Crewe. Since its' introduction as No. D1743 in June 1964, it was allocated to all the regions except the Southern. No. 47150 appeared in February 1974, and then 47399 in March 1994, but it returned to 47150 in September 1995. It was withdrawn by Freightliner in July 2007.
Gavin Morrison

Date 29th September 2002
In 2001 Chris Green Chief Executive of Virgin Trains sanctioned the painting of 5 class 47/8's to be repainted from Virgin Livery into the ex BR Liveries, although 47826 wasn't repainted it remained in Inter-City Swallow Livery. This was extremely popular with enthusiasts around the country, and probably the most interesting was 47853's appearance in the XP64 livery, which it actually carried when it was numbered D1733. Here we see it recovering from a signal check outside Stockport Station whilst heading the diverted 1A60, 16.10 Liverpool-Milton Keynes, (the line was closed to Euston). When it received the XP64 livery it was also named 'Rail Express Magazine', which took place at Grosmont on the North Yorkshire Moors railway on 27th April 2002. It joined the Riviera Trains fleet on 23 October 2002 and saw some use, but has not been out on the main line for some time and is still at Crewe. It carried the No. 47141 from February 1974 until becoming 47614 in July 1984 and 47853 in March 1990.
Gavin Morrison

Date 14 June 2003
In 2002 and 2003 EWS gave 10 Class 47/7's major overhauls and repainted them in their very attractive Red livery, one of the 10 was No. 47792 which had been named 'Robin Hood' in March 2003 is seen at Great Brington heading the 13.15 Euston-Liverpool. It is in immaculate condition and probably had only recently received its' overhaul at Toton depot. It carried many names and identities starting with D1965 in October 1965. No. 47265 followed in February 1974 and then 47591 in July 1983 whilst part of Inter-City it became 47804 and then 47792 in March 1995. The name 'Kettering' was attached in September 1992 and removed in August 1993. 'Saint Cuthbert' followed in May 1995 and finally 'Robin Hood' plates in March 2003. It is now an active member of the West Coast Railway Companies fleet.
Gavin Morrison

Date 1 November 2003
The usual West Coast diversions were taking place in the Autumn of 2003 from Preston to Crewe via Stockport. By a stroke of good fortune 2 of the ex First Great Western liveried 47/8's Nos. 47830 and 47816 were on the duties and appeared double headed on a Glasgow-Euston service in the afternoon at Bolton, where they are seen passing through the station. Details about 47830 are on page 19, whereas No. 47816 entered service in January 1965 as D1650, became 47066 in January 1964, then 47661 in December 1986 and finally 47816 in February 1989. It only carried the name 'Bristol Bath Road Quality Approved' from May 1995 to December 2002. It was eventually withdrawn by Freightliner in January 2008.

Gavin Morrison

Date 5 September 2004
More West Coast diversions, this time it is Virgin No. 47805 dragging Class 87 No. 87033 past Winwick Junction just north of Warrington on the IF18 15.57 Stafford to Liverpool Lime Street. It started its' career on the Western Region in March 1966 as No. D1935, then changed to 47257 in June 1974 followed by 47650 in July 1986 and finally 47805 in August 1989. It carried 3 names starting with Bristol Bath Road from June 1991 to February 1995. 'Prince of Toton' followed in February 2002 to July 2005 and after joining the Riviera 47 fleet it became 'Talisman' in October 2006. It is currently based at Crewe. Note it is carrying a Freightliner sticker on the cab side.
Gavin Morrison

(*Top Left*)

Date 2 April 2005

The history of No. 47832 has been given on page 57. Around this period it was generally to be found making a daily return trip along the North Wales coast, covering for the troublesome Class 175 dmu's run by First group. It still retained the First Great Western green livery but the branding was replaced by 'Fragonset'. It is seen in this picture working a special, 1Z47 from Norwich to Buxton past Grindleford in the Hope Valley. Today it looks much smarter in its' DRS Company livery. *Gavin Morrison*

(*Bottom*)

Date 29th July 2005

The annual airshow at Lowestoft produces locomotive hauled extras from Norwich each year No. 47714 in its' distinctive and unique Anglia livery for a class 47 is shown alongside one of the Norfolk Broads at Haddiscoe heading the 18.00 from Lowestoft to Norwich. It entered service in November 1966 numbered D1955, change to 47511 in March 1974 and then 47714 in March 1985. It carried the name 'Thames' from March 1979 to September 1984, and then after it joined the Scottish push/pull fleet, was named 'Grampian Region' in May 1985 till February 1989 when it then headed south to join the Network South East fleet. It was withdrawn in August 1996 and stored, until eventually sold to Cotswold Rail in December 2001. It was then put to work as the 'Anglia' thunderbird based at Norwich. Upon the demise of Cotswold Road it was bought by Harry Needle Railroad Company, where it is still operational (2010) but not on the national network. *Gavin Morrison*

Date 10 June 2006
No. 47832 is seen again in yet another livery. This one was the result of the merger of Fragonset Railways and Merlin Rail, which unfortunately was very short lived. It is shown here carrying the name 'Driver Tom Clarke OBE' at the rear of a Pathfinder special passing Woodhouse to the east of Sheffield, having started at Ealing Broadway and visited Barrow Hill, and was heading to Deepcar when this picture was taken. Details on 47832 are given on page 57. *Gavin Morrison*

Date 3 September 2005
No. 47355 became the property of Fragonset Railways at the end of 2001. It was repainted into this livery which was the Fragonset freight livery. From time to time it was out on passenger workings as seen here where it is on the rear of special 5Z47 Norwich to Carlisle passing Lostock Junction, the train being hauled by Fragonset Class 47/7 No. 47709. No. 47355 was new as No. D1836 in May 1965 and changed to 47355 in March 1974. In April it became 47391 and reverted to 47355 in September 1995. It carried the name Avocet between November 2002 and January 2007. The locomotive is currently stored at West Coast Carnforth, and is expected to return to traffic in the near future. *Gavin Morrison*

Date 6 June 2006
Whilst under the Fragonset ownership the ex Tinsley pet loco No. 47145 'Merddin Emrys' is shown hauling a special No. 1Z32, the 16.40 Carlisle-Norwich past Hunslet in the south suburb's of Leeds. Details of the locomotive are given on page 40, but during the 13 years since the picture on page 40 was taken and this picture, it was repainted into a darker blue and had the Railfreight distribution decals on the body sides plus a crest on the cabside. It was scrapped during 2009.

Date 15th July 2006
F.M.Rail decided in 1996 that there was sufficient demand to introduce another luxury Pullman train into the market. With a set of MK2 coaches (air conditioned) plus 2 MK1 Kitchen buffet cars. The train was painted in a very attractive Nanking Blue livery, as were 2 of their class 47/7's Nos. 47709 'Dionyss' and 47712 'Artemis', the whole train presented a very pleasing sight. Several trips were run, but apparently did not make enough money and the stock ended up with West Coast Rail at Carnforth, and the 47/7's in the DRS fleet, where they are both active. No. 47709 is shown leaving Llandudno for Euston with 47712 on the rear. *Gavin Morrison*

Date 24 July 2006
Towards the end of July 2006 special workings were organised between Carnforth and Carlisle, with 2 return trips per day for driver training. West Coast Railways provided the coaches and DRS Class 47's. No. 47501, un-named and in the first DRS livery for their class 47's is heading south round the curve at Low Gill heading for Carnforth.

It was new as No. D1944 in July 1966 and has only changed numbers once when it became No. 47501 in February 1974. It carried the name 'Craftsman' from October 1987 until June 1990, but it was refitted again 1 month later, they were again removed in September 1997, when the locomotive was stored. It was sold to Brailsworth Engineering in August 2001 to operate under the Fragonset Banner, but in the end was sold to DRS, overhauled at Alstom Traincare Glasgow and is now operational in the DRS fleet. *Gavin Morrison*

Date 9th September 2006
After the demise of 'Anglia', the franchise was taken over by National Express. Cotswold Rail had the contract for dragging Class 90's and their stock in the summer from Norwich to Great Yarmouth. No. 47818 named 'Emily' (April 2008) was painted in the extraordinarily named ONE franchise livery. Here it is seen carrying out its dragging duties as it hauls Class 90 No. 90014 and its' stock into Great Yarmouth. DRS has now taken over these duties, and 47818 is now owned by Harry Needle but not certified for the network. No. 47818 was new in December 1965 and numbered D1917, then it received No. 47240 in November 1973 followed by 47663 in January 1987 and finally 47818 in February 1989. The name 'Strathclyde' was carried between September 2000 and March 2003.
Gavin Morrison

Date 28th September 2006
Yet another livery carried by a few Class 47's to pass into history, this time Cotswold Rail, which had a small fleet of 47's together with its' freight Co. Advenza Rail which also had 57's. Both companies went out of business in October 2009, with their locomotives sold on, mainly to Harry Needle Railroad Co.

No. 47813, named John Peel between October 2005 on March 2009 is shown leaving Healey Mills yard (now closed) heading special working 6Z47 to Gloucester.

It was new in March 1964 as No. D1720, changed to 47129 in February 1974, 47658 followed in October 1986 and then 47813 in July 1989. It was named 'SS Great Britain' in April 1988 which it carried until May 2003. It is not currently (2010) main line certified.

Gavin Morrison

Date 14th June 2008
A Compass Tours special, No. 1Z86, 5.50 Runcorn-Edinburgh with Riviera Class 47/8's Nos. 47843 and 47815 (in BR green) head through the Calder Valley at Eastwood (west of Hebden Bridge) with No. 47843 in its' plain but pleasant blue livery and carrying the name 'Pegasus'. It carried the name 'Vulcan' from October 1965, these were temporarily removed whilst the loco was stored June 1989 and reinstated in August 2000. Sadly the Riviera fleet of Class 47's see little or no work currently, which is a shame as they painted in attractive different liveries.

Gavin Morrison

Date 26th July 2008
As mentioned in the captions on page 51 it was virtually unknown for locomotives to carry advertising in BR days, but since privatisation there have been the occasional exceptions. One of these was when West Coast Railways No. 47826 was adorned with this Scarborough Spa Express advert, which contained an excellent picture of the companies Stanier 8F No. 48151. It was selected as the back-up locomotive for the S.S.E., and therefore spent most of the summer at York station, where it could be easily seen. It was only done on one side, and presumably it contributed to the success of the special train over the last few years. No. 47826's brief history is given on page 28. The Ferris Wheel which was installed at the NRM, and which was also a great success can be seen above the locomotive.
Gavin Morrison

Date 18th November 2008
No. 47237 is seen here in the Advenza blue livery passing Burton Salmon hauling a dead No. 47145 back to Gloucester in a Stockton to Cardiff scrap train. The history of No. 47237 has been given on page 38 and No. 47145 on pages 40 and 47.
Gavin Morrison

Date 24th August 2007
Prior to the start of Grand Central services between Sunderland and Kings Cross, the company hired DRS (Direct Rail Services) Class 47's to carry out driver training. On a glorious summers afternoon No. 47802 with No. 47237 on the rear is heading north at Dawdon which is just south of Seaham in the North East.

The locomotive was built at Brush Traction in September 1966, entering service as No. D1950. No. 47259 followed in March 1974, then No. 47552 in February 1975 and finally No. 47802 in July 1989. It was bought by DRS in May 2002 for spares from Alston but was repaired and is still currently active. It was named 'Pride of Cumbria' in February 2008.

Gavin Morrison

Date 11 September 2009
Empty stock movements from the West Coast Railway Co. at Carnforth to various starting points in the east of the country have now become nothing unusual. Very often they pass through Leeds station heading east, and here No. 47245 (with 47760 on the rear) is heading train 5Z70, the 9.55 Carnforth to Doncaster, seen passing Osmanthorpe to the east of Leeds near Cross Gates.

No. 47245 was new as D1922 in December 1965, becoming 47245 in October 1973. It carried the uninspiring name the 'Institute of Export' from July 1994 to January 1999, when it was withdrawn. It remained in store until February 2003 when it was moved to the Barrow Hill Museum. Currently it is the only active Class 47/0 in the West Coast Fleet.

Gavin Morrison